SUZE ORMAN

THE ULTIMATE PROTECTION PORTFOLIO™

Estate Planning Documents

This product provides information and general advice about the law. But laws and procedures change frequently, and they can be interpreted differently by different people. For specific advice geared to your specific situation, consult an expert. No book, software, or other published material is a substitute for personalized advice from a knowledgeable lawyer licensed to practice law in your state.

HAY HOUSE, INC.
Carlsbad, California • New York City
London • Sydney • Johannesburg
Vancouver • Hong Kong

Published and distributed in the United States by Hay House, Inc., P.O. Box 5100, Carlsbad, CA 92018-5100 • *Phone:* (760) 431-7695 or (800) 654-5126 • *Fax:* (760) 431-6948 or (800) 650-5115 • www.hayhouse.com®

ISBN 13: 978-1-4019-0345-9
ISBN 1-4019-0345-2

11 10 09 08   7 6 5 4
1st printing, November 2003
4th printing, May 2008

Printed in China

Estate Planning Documents

Please locate the documents listed in the "Estate Planning Documents Checklist" below and file each of them in your Protection Portfolio.

ESTATE PLANNING DOCUMENTS CHECKLIST

- ☐ Advanced directive and durable power of attorney for health care
- ☐ Financial durable power of attorney
- ☐ Will
- ☐ Pour over will
- ☐ Revocable living trust
- ☐ Contracts for funeral or memorial arrangements, and documentation of prepaid fees to cemetery and/or funeral home

You may not have all the documents listed here, so this booklet (along with the Protection Portfolio CD-ROM) is intended to help you obtain and complete them. But even if you already have them, I strongly urge you to listen to the audio clips on the CD-ROM to make sure you have the correct documents in place and that you truly understand the uses and ramifications of each one of them. Whenever you sign your name to any legal document, it's essential that you know what every clause means. This is the reason I created the CD-ROM.

Advanced Directive and Durable Power of Attorney for Health Care

The Importance of the Advanced Directive
and Durable Power of Attorney for Health Care

As far as I'm concerned, the advanced directive and durable power of attorney for health care is the single most important document that you need to have in your portfolio. Most of the other documents that we'll be discussing are intended more for the benefit of your heirs and the people you leave behind after you die. But this one is for you.

I hope that you won't ever be incapacitated or hospitalized, and that a long, healthy life awaits you. But just in case, I urge you to make the simple arrangements for an advanced directive and durable power of attorney for health care. Do this for yourself and for the people you love, and do it now, while you're strong and healthy. It might be the most important document you ever sign.

The advanced directive and durable power of attorney for health care directly affects the quality of your life and the quality of your death—that is, the manner in which you leave this world. The right to die, which means the right not to be put on life support, is something we've only had in the United States since 1990, and it's a right explicitly granted to us in decisions by the U.S. Supreme Court. Since that time, however, courts in different states have made it clear that unless you put your wishes in writing, a doctor doesn't have to unplug you from life support—no matter how devastated your body is, no matter how much competency you've lost, no matter how much of a vegetable you've become from whatever it is that has befallen you.

The reason this should be important to you—not only emotionally, but financially—is that most health-insurance policies put a cap on the maximum amount they'll pay for an illness. This maximum varies from policy to policy, but the average is about $1 million. So, after your insurance company has paid out about $1 million in benefits, it's done. The rest is up to you and your loved ones. With the cost of hospitalization skyrocketing, I'm sure you can imagine that it wouldn't take long to reach the maximum if you happened to be on a life-support system in a hospital. And yet the medical bills would keep piling up. Having an advanced health care directive and durable power of attorney for health care is part of being responsible to your family, not only on an emotional level, but on a financial level as well.

On your Protection Portfolio CD-ROM, you'll find an advanced directive and power of attorney for health care document that you can customize to use in any state. You'll also find a link to Caring Connections, a program of the National Hospice and Palliative Care Organization (NHPCO), where you can print out copies of your own state's forms. Forms can also be procured at most hospitals or public health services in your area.

Advanced Directive for Health Care Section

Also known as a living will, a directive to physicians, a health-care declaration, an advanced health-care directive, or a medical directive, the advanced directive for health care is a written document that dictates what you want to have happen to you if you're incapacitated. You can choose from three basic options:

1. You want to prolong your life for as long as possible, without regard to your condition, your chance of recovery, or the cost of treatment.

2. You want life-sustaining treatment to be provided unless you're in a coma or an ongoing vegetative state.

3. You don't want your life to be prolonged un-
naturally, unless there is some hope that both
your physical and mental health might be
restored.

Durable Power of Attorney for Health Care Section

A durable power of attorney for health care (which may also
be called a medical power of attorney, a health-care proxy, or an
appointment of health-care agent or surrogate) is a document
that designates someone who will have the authority to make
health-care decisions for you if you're unable to due to an incapacity. The person appointed may be called a health-care agent,
surrogate, an attorney in-fact, or a proxy. (In Nebraska, he or
she must be at least 19. In all other states, the agent must be 18
or older.)

In the durable power of attorney for health care, you must
decide in whose hands you want to put your life—that is, who
will make the final decision to take you off life support, if the
decision ever has to be made. It's best to have an agent and two
alternates, in case the person you've chosen isn't available.
Choose people who love you, yet are strong enough to do what
you would want them to do. This isn't an easy position to be in.

I want you to take a moment to consider whom you'd want
to be the agent and alternates for your durable power of attorney. This is one of the most important decisions you'll make,
so please don't rush into it. Give it some careful thought, and
when you've made up your mind, write the names of your
choices in the following box.

AGENT AND ALTERNATES FOR DURABLE POWER OF ATTORNEY FOR HEALTH CARE

I will ask _____ to be my agent for my durable power of attorney for health care.

I will ask _____ to be an alternate agent for my durable power of attorney for health care.

I will ask _____ to be an alternate agent for my durable power of attorney for health care.

Once you've decided whom you want to ask, get in touch with your chosen agent and alternates and find a time when you can discuss your decision with them in private. As difficult as this conversation may be, please don't put off this step. The moment you need this document, it's too late to create it.

Common Questions about the Advanced Directive and Durable Power of Attorney for Health Care

In the following section, I've answered the questions I'm most often asked about the Advanced Directive and Durable Power of Attorney for Health Care.

- *I already have a living will. Do I still need the durable power of attorney for health care?* Yes, because a living will (also known as an advanced directive) and a durable power of attorney have different purposes. In the document provided on your Protection Portfolio CD-ROM, the advanced directive and durable power of attorney are combined into one document. The durable power of attorney for health care allows you to designate a person who can make the decision to take you off life support (and dictate under what circumstances) and to make less drastic medical decisions, too. An advanced directive, on the other hand, gives guidance to a doctor as to what types of treatments you'd want, but it doesn't authorize anyone to make decisions for you. The durable power of attorney for health care shifts the decision-making power from the doctor to your agent as soon as your doctor determines that you're no longer able to make decisions for yourself (for example, if you were unconscious or delirious). You can tell your agent your preferences for treatment, but if there are unexpected circumstances, the agent won't be locked into what was written in a directive years before.

- *If there aren't any circumstances under which I'd want to be taken off life support, then I don't need to bother with the durable power of attorney, right?* Quite the contrary—you can state in your durable power of attorney for health care that you want heroic measures taken to save your life, no matter what kind of prognosis you might have for recovery. That's the point of the durable health power of attorney—it lets your family and your doctors know definitively what your wishes are, if and when you can't communicate them.

- *What should I keep in mind when selecting an agent for my durable power of attorney for health care?* Whomever you select as your agent must be strong enough to act in accordance with your wishes, even if your loved ones strongly disagree. You should choose someone you have confidence in, who lives no more than a day's travel away, and with whom you've discussed your preferences for health care. Also consider whether your agent has too much of a conflict of interest (if, say, the person who can authorize pulling the plug also stands to inherit a lot of money from you). If the person you're considering has any hesitation about acting in that role, you should appoint someone else. If possible, it's also wise to appoint several alternate agents.

- *Can I make both of my daughters co-agents on my durable power of attorney for health care?* The document provided on the Protection Portfolio CD-ROM doesn't allow co-agents. Here's why: Even if you're very specific about your wishes, your agents will probably have a lot of discretion to determine whether your medical circumstances meet the qualifications for carrying out your instructions. If your co-agents were to disagree with each other about anything, it's likely that no action would be taken, thus making all your planning worthless. In most cases, your child will consult with his or her siblings anyway, and you can express ahead of time your preference that he or she do so.

  The document provided on the CD-ROM does give you the ability to make your other children alternate agents. This means that you'd have a second or third alternate agent if your first agent were unavailable for any reason.

- *If I want to change the agent I designated on my durable power of attorney for health care, what should I do?* Included on your Protection Portfolio CD-ROM is a document to revoke a durable power of attorney for health care. If your circumstances ever change, and you decide that you actually want to revoke the person you've appointed as your agent, you can do so simply by using this revocation document. Fill in the revocation document and then deliver a copy to every person and institution that had a copy of your original durable power of attorney for health care.

  Providing the institutions with the revocation document is the only way for them to know that your previous durable power of attorney for health care is no longer valid. If, in fact, you do this, know that you no longer now have a durable power of attorney for health care in place, so you'll have to create another one. This can easily be done using the advanced directive and durable power of attorney form provided on your Protection Portfolio CD-ROM. Please make sure you keep both the revocation and your revised advanced directive and durable power of attorney for health care in your Protection Portfolio.

- *Once I draw up my advanced directive and durable power of attorney for health care, is it good forever?* Yes, although you can and should revoke it and create a new one if the person whom you appointed as your agent dies, you decide to appoint a different agent, or you change your mind about what kind of medical treatment you'd want in dire circumstances.

- *If an advanced directive and durable power of attorney for health care is such an important document, why don't more people have one?* I think the answer to this question is that so many of us are simply afraid to confront our own mortality. Signing a paper such as this makes death seem like an imminent reality, and that can provoke frightening and painful feelings. Another reason people don't sign such a power of attorney is they think they're too young to contemplate such things. But I promise you, no matter what your age, this is one of the most important things you can do to protect yourself and your finances.

- *Where should I store my advanced directive and durable power of attorney for health care?* You should always keep the original in your Protection Portfolio. Give a copy of the form to the person you've chosen to act as your agent, and send copies to your doctor and your health-insurance company to be kept as part of your medical records.

Financial Power of Attorney

Financial Power of Attorney

A financial power of attorney is a document that authorizes another person to act for you as if that person were you. This person is called your *agent* or your *attorney-in-fact*. You can create a very broad power of attorney, which allows your agent to do things that usually only you can do, such as write checks from your bank accounts, pay your bills, or sign documents on your behalf. Alternately, you can create a very limited power of attorney, which may authorize the agent you name to do just one particular thing for you.

In my opinion, the best power of attorney is one that is: (1) authorized by a specific state law (also known as a statutory power of attorney); (2) is a general power of attorney; and (3) survives the incapacity of the maker. These three factors will give you the greatest ease in getting people and institutions to cooperate with you when you transact business through a power of attorney. Finally, your power of attorney needs to be "durable" to remain in effect if you become incapacitated. This is the main reason for any power of attorney.

Keep in mind, however, that a general power of attorney has been called a "license to steal," since it's like signing a blank check. Also, certain institutions may refuse to honor your power of attorney if it's not in the form the institution itself prefers— even if it's a statutory form.

> ### *Explanation of the Use of California Probate Code*
>
> You may have noticed that the financial power of attorney on your Protection Portfolio CD-ROM is labeled "California Probate Code Section 4401." The fact that the document is a California statutory power of attorney doesn't mean that it won't be valid in other states — it's valid in all 50 states and will protect you no matter what state you happen to live in. The reason that I chose to provide you with a form governed under the California Probate Code is that California has a specific piece of legislation that makes it possible for you to sue an institution — and have your attorney's fees paid by that institution — if the institution refuses to honor the power of attorney, causing you damages. This is a very persuasive element, and it has made the difference between having this document accepted or not accepted in some important circumstances.

Common Questions about the Financial Power of Attorney

In the following section, I've answered the questions I'm most often asked about Financial Power of Attorney.

- *Can an institution refuse to honor my financial power of attorney?* Yes. Because powers of attorney are so easily abused, certain institutions may refuse to honor one if it's not on the form the institution itself prints—even if it's a statutory form. For example, the IRS requires you to complete their transmittal Form 2848 in order to process any non-IRS power of attorney.

  Also, if you try to limit the scope of the power of attorney or make it too specific, brokerage houses may not want to accept it because they feel it doesn't cover all the types of actions they deem necessary.

- *What's the difference between a power of attorney and a durable power of attorney?* A power of attorney authorizes someone to make legal and financial decisions on your behalf while you're alive. But, generally, if you become incapacitated, the power of attorney becomes void. A *durable* power of attorney stays in effect even after you're incapacitated, which is when you really need someone you trust making decisions for you. The financial power of attorney included on the Protection Portfolio CD-ROM is a durable power of attorney.

- *What happens to your financial power of attorney upon your death?* After you die, the power of attorney is no longer effective, and your agent should not try to transact any business for you then—he or she can no longer legally sign anything as your agent. Such an act constitutes an ethical breach that could be used against your agent if there were any disputes with heirs, creditors, or the IRS.

- *How should an agent (attorney-in-fact) sign documents and checks?* If your name is John Smith and your agent (the person signing for you) is Mary Smith, then she would sign as follows: *John Smith by his attorney in fact Mary Smith.*
  After you die, the power of attorney is no longer effective, and your agent should not try to transact *any* business for you then.

- *If I want to change the person I've designated as my agent (attorney-in-fact), what do I need to do?*

Included on your Protection Portfolio CD-ROM is a document to revoke a financial power of attorney. If you decide that the agent you've appointed is no longer someone that you'd want to act in that capacity, then fill in the revocation form and deliver it to every person and institution that originally had a copy of the financial power of attorney.

Providing the institutions with your revocation document is the only way for them to know that your previous financial power of attorney is no longer valid. If you do this, you'll no longer have a financial power of attorney in place. You'll have to create a new one, which can easily be done using the financial power of attorney document provided on you Protection Portfolio CD-ROM.

- *Where should I store my financial power of attorney?* Since this document grants another individual the ability to make financial decisions for you, it isn't something you want to give out until it's absolutely necessary. I recommend that you simply keep the document and all copies of it in your Protection Portfolio. Then tell your attorney-in-fact that should something happen to you that causes you to be incapacitated or unable to take care of your financial matters, he or she can find the document granting financial power of attorney in your Protection Portfolio. This way, if you do decide to revoke the financial power of attorney in the future, you don't have multiple financial powers of attorney on file with different financial institutions.

will

Your Will

One of the most important steps in being responsible to yourself and others is to make sure that you have a will. Of course, thinking about your death or the death of a family member is no easy assignment, and neither is contemplating a serious illness or incapacity. But planning for the future can, and probably will, give you a sense of control over your life. It's freeing to know that you've protected those you care most about.

A will is a legal document that states where you want your assets to go after your death. However, the title to your property won't automatically transfer to your designated beneficiary after your death. Your will must be "probated" in court, which is a lengthy and costly procedure.

Probate is a court procedure in which the judge first has to authenticate your will and make sure it's valid, then sign a court order to transfer your property over to your beneficiaries. This sounds simple, but in some states it can take six months to two years to complete the process, and it can be quite expensive. Take California, for example:

Estate Size	Probate Fee, California*
$100,000	$8,000
$200,000	$14,000
$300,000	$18,000
$400,000	$22,000
$500,000	$26,000
$600,000	$30,000
$1,000,000	$46,000

*Combined basic fees for executor and attorney.

If your estate is small, from $5,000 to $100,000 (depending on the state), you might be able to avoid probate with a simple will and a process called *probate affidavit*. It costs very little, doesn't take much time, and makes it easy for your survivors to receive what you want them to have. Probate affidavit forms are available from most banks at no cost. Be careful, though—your estate could be worth more than you think.

I urge you to discuss your estate—the sum total of your property and money—with your spouse or life partner, with your children, and with anyone else who will be financially affected by your death. Also, if you're married or hold joint assets with someone else, please take time now to learn everything you can about your joint finances, so that if you're the one left behind, you won't have to cope with financial confusion on top of your grief. On your Protection Portfolio CD-ROM, you'll find a will that you can customize to fit your individual needs.

TERMINOLOGY OF WILLS

TERM	DEFINITION
Administrator	When there is no will, this is the person who is appointed by the probate court to collect the assets of the estate, pay its debts, and distribute the rest to beneficiaries.
Beneficiary	A person or organization designated to receive your assets upon your death.
Estate	The sum total of your financial interests, both money and property. Your estate is made up of everything you own at the time of your death, including life insurance, less your outstanding debt.
Executor	The person you appoint in your will to settle your estate. This person will have the administrative responsibility of paying your bills, dealing with the probate court, supervising the process of securing your assets, and making sure your wishes are carried out.
Testator	The person who created the will.

In addition to the information supplied on the CD-ROM, I've listed the following will benefit statement definitions in this guidebook to help you make the choice on how you want your assets distributed (these choices will be presented on the CD-ROM program when you create your will).

WILL BENEFICIARY STATEMENT DEFINITIONS

TERM	DEFINITION
Right of Representation	This statement means that if the beneficiary you've named dies before you do, then you want the share that beneficiary would have taken to go to their child, children, or lineal descendants.
Equal Shares to Lapse	This statement means that if one of the beneficiaries dies before you, then their share goes away—it doesn't go to their children. So if you give equal shares to seven nieces and nephews and one dies before you, then there will just be six shares, even if the deceased nephew had his own children.
Percentages	This statement means that you can choose to distribute your estate in amounts designated by percentages. This allows you to distribute your estate into equal or unequal shares and between individuals and organizations.
Specific Gifts	This statement allows a beneficiary to be named to receive a specific gift, such as your home. Specific gifts are usually not the best idea—since most people don't know when they're going to die, there may be unintended consequences when leaving a specific asset to someone. The asset may have been sold before you die leaving the beneficiary with nothing. You may have spent all your other assets, leaving other beneficiaries with nothing. However, there are cases where it's very clear that a specific asset should be given to a specific beneficiary.

Common Questions about Wills

In the following section, I've listed the questions I'm most often asked about wills, along with the answers.

- *How do I get a will?* There are a few ways you can do this. First, you can have a lawyer draw one up. This should cost from a couple hundred to a thousand dollars, depending on where you live and how complex your affairs are. You can also buy a form will (which should cost about $10 at a stationery store) and fill in the blanks. Or you can complete and print out the will on your Protection Portfolio CD-ROM.

  If you use any of these methods to draw up your will, you'll also need to sign it, and while you're signing it, have two people witness your signature (unless you live in Vermont, which requires three witnesses). Your witnesses will then need to sign the will, too. If you live in Louisiana, you must sign the bottom of each page of your will in addition to signing the signature page in order for your will to be valid.

- *Who can witness a will?* A witness must be an adult who won't be receiving any gifts in the will. And it's best if a witness isn't related to you.

- *What if I want to make changes to my will?* Instead of creating a codicil to your will, I recommend that you use the Protection Portfolio to create a new, updated will, incorporating the changes you want at this time. This ensures that all of your wishes are contained in a single document.

- *What's a holographic will?* A holographic will is a will you write by hand on a piece of paper. It costs you nothing. Just make sure that the paper you use has no other writing on it, or the will won't be considered legal. The entire will needs to be in your handwriting and dated and signed *by you.* If you make a mistake, don't cross it out—start over. Anything crossed out makes the will null and void. Don't have anyone witness a holographic will because, again, this will make it null and void. If you want to change a holographic will, you must redo the entire thing. Holographic wills aren't legal in every state.

- *Can wills be contested?* Yes. Anyone who thinks that he or she should have something that the deceased left to someone else in the will has the right to come to court and ask for it. Then the judge has to decide. Also, although people commonly use wills to designate the guardians they want for their children, their recommendation isn't binding. It can only express a wish.

- *How old do I have to be to have a will?* In most states, you need to be 18 years old or older to make a will. If you're younger than this and think you need a will, see an attorney.

- *Can I leave assets to beneficiaries other than my spouse and children?* If you want to leave more than half of your estate to someone other than your spouse, see a lawyer. If you have no spouse and you want to leave more than half of your estate to someone other than your children, see a lawyer.

OWNERSHIP ISSUES THAT AFFECT PROPERTY LEFT BY A WILL

TYPE OF OWNERSHIP	RULES FOR LEAVING PROPERTY
Co-owned property, such as real estate, cars, securities, small businesses, and copyrights	If you co-own property, you need to figure out the percentage you own and whether you have the right to gift it to someone else. See the chart on the next page called "Rules for Co-owned Property."
Property with named beneficiaries, such as life insurance, retirement plans, bank accounts, and living trusts	If you named a beneficiary on your account or policy, then the asset will be distributed to the individual you named— not the beneficiary you named in your will. Please check all your accounts to make sure you have the correct beneficiary listed.
Property controlled by contract, such as partnership interest or stock in a corporation controlled by shareholder approval	Most contracts dictate how these properties are distributed, and in a dispute, the contract supersedes your will. See a lawyer if you want to distribute your property differently than is specified in your contract.

RULES FOR CO-OWNED PROPERTY

HOW PROPERTY IS HELD	RULES FOR LEAVING PROPERTY
Tenancy in Common	You can give away your share of property unless a different beneficiary is in place, you're restricted by a contract, or martial-ownership laws forbid your doing so. (See charts "Rules for Married People in Community-Property States" and "Rules for Married People in Common-Law Property States" on pages 29 and 30 of this booklet.)
Joint Tenancy (also called Joint Tenancy with Right of Survivorship)	You can't give away your share of joint-tenancy property. It automatically goes to any surviving joint tenants. You may still include joint-tenancy property in your will to prepare for the possibility that: (1) The entire property ends up in your estate because the other joint tenant dies before you; or (2) the property is converted to tenancy in common.
Tenancy by the Entirety	You can't give away your share of property held in tenancy by the entirety. It automatically goes to your spouse. You may still include tenancy by the entirety property in your will to prepare for the possibility that: (1) The entire property ends up in your estate because your spouse dies before you; or (2) the property is converted to tenancy in common.

- *Can I leave assets to young beneficiaries?* Most states allow you to leave assets for young people to a custodian to manage until the young person is between 18 and 25, depending on the state. This is called the Uniform Transfers to Minors Act and it appears in the will provided on your Protection Portfolio CD-ROM. Since you can't change the age at which the young person gets the money (as it's set by law), the form uses the maximum age. There are only two states that don't allow this: South Carolina and Vermont. If you're concerned about young beneficiaries in these states, use a trust instead of a will.

- *What if I don't have a will?* The answer is that you *do* have a will, whether you know it or not. Even if you haven't personally drawn up a will, the state you live in has something called *intestate succession rules*. These rules determine exactly who receives any assets held in your name when you die without a written will. Usually, your spouse and children receive your property first. If you aren't survived by a spouse or children, your grandchildren might be next in line, followed by your parents, siblings, nieces, nephews, and cousins. If you die without any relatives whom anyone can find, your assets will pass to the state.

RULES FOR MARRIED PEOPLE IN COMMUNITY-PROPERTY STATES
(ARIZONA, CALIFORNIA, IDAHO, NEVADA, NEW MEXICO, TEXAS, WASHINGTON, AND WISCONSIN)

HOW PROPERTY IS OWNED	RULES FOR LEAVING PROPERTY
Separately	You can give away your separate property, except in the following cases: • The property is held in joint tenancy • The property has a beneficiary designation • The property is restricted from transfer by a contract
Community Property	You can give away your half of community property, except in the following cases: • The property is held in joint tenancy • The property has a different beneficiary designated on the account or policy • The property is restricted from transfer by a contract

RULES FOR MARRIED PEOPLE IN COMMON-LAW STATES
(ALL STATES EXCEPT ARIZONA, CALIFORNIA, IDAHO, NEVADA, NEW MEXICO, TEXAS, WASHINGTON, AND WISCONSIN)

HOW PROPERTY IS OWNED	RULES FOR LEAVING PROPERTY
Separate Property	You can give away your separate property, except in the following cases: • The property is held in joint tenancy • The property is held in tenancy by the entirety • The property has a different beneficiary designated on the account or policy • The property is restricted from transfer by a contract
Marital Property	You can give away your share of jointly owned property, except in the following cases: • The property is held in joint tenancy • The property is held in tenancy by the entirety • The property has a different beneficiary designated on the account or policy • The property is restricted from transfer by a contract

For additional information about wills, you can also visit the resource center at my Website, *www.suzeorman.com.*

Pour Over Will

Later on, I'm going to ask you to consider whether you need a revocable living trust, and then I'll provide direction on how to draw one up. Even if you have a trust, however, you still need a will.

When you have a revocable living trust, your will takes the form of a "pour over will." What this means is that any assets not owned by you as a trustee of your trust when you die can be added to the trust, or "poured over" by your will into your trust. A pour over will covers anything you may have left out of your trust by mistake.

If you don't have a revocable living trust, you'd simply use a standard will, rather than a pour over will.

Will Affidavit

In the past, after you died, in order to prove that a will was valid, the witnesses who signed the will had to come to probate court to testify to the fact that they saw you sign your will. Now, in most states, signing such an affidavit can be done ahead of time, at the signing of the will, so that witnesses don't need to be called in to court. However, in Washington, D.C.; Maryland; and Vermont, witnesses can't sign in advance, so you'll want to make sure that your executor has their contact information in case there's a need to go to court after your death. In California, Ohio, and Michigan, you don't need to fill out an affidavit—the will is all that's needed. For all other states, an appropriate will affidavit has been provided on your Protection Portfolio CD-ROM.

When you fill in your personal information on the CD-ROM to create a will, if you need a will affidavit, the program will alert you and provide the appropriate form based on the state you live in.

How to Change Tangible Personal Property in Your Will

To avoid having to redo your will every time you change your mind about who you want to receive certain items of personal property, you can simply write a letter to the executor of your will instructing him or her of the change. Following, you'll find an example of this informal way of writing a letter to your will's executor. If you write directions in your own handwriting, it makes your letter a stronger statement. Typically, you'll direct some of your possessions to specific people; almost never will you direct the disposition of each and every thing.

Tangible personal property includes your furniture, jewelry, artwork, personal papers, cars, tools, clothes, computers, appliances, cameras, electronic equipment, pets, and so on.

Sample Letter to an Executor to Add or Change Personal Property

February 15, 2005

Dear Mr. Smith, executor of my will dated_____:

Please give my 1956 Chevrolet car to my grandson John Smith.

Please give my wedding ring, gold jewelry, and watch to my daughter Mary.

Please give my tools and computers to my son John.

Please give my collection of china and crystal to my friend Linda Smith.

Yours,

_____Name

_____Signature

Revocable Living Trust

Revocable Living Trusts

Of all the documents I've ever talked to you about, of all the things you've ever heard me mention on TV or in any book, a revocable living trust is the document I've probably most often said is indispensable. It's certainly one of the most important documents you can have to protect yourself.

On the Protection Portfolio CD-ROM, I've included a revocable living trust for you to personalize, based on your individual situation. After you listen to the information about trusts on the CD-ROM, you may have additional questions. The following section is an added resource devoted to what you need to know about trusts.

Explanation of the Use of a California Trust

You may have noticed that the trust on your Protection Portfolio CD-ROM provides that it's governed by the laws of the state of California. This means that no matter what state you live in, California law will be applied to the interpretation of your trust. California trust law is very modern and user friendly, and the laws of California are more favorable to the consumer than those of any other state, in my opinion.

The reason that your trust is valid in your home state, even though it's governed by California law, is based on the same laws that allow a person to incorporate in Delaware even if they've never set foot in that state. The specifics of this principle are found in section 268(1) of the *Restatement of the Law Second, Conflict Laws,* (St. Paul, Minn.: American Law Institute Publishers, 1969) which states:

> "As with testamentary trusts, a settlor may designate which state's local law will govern construction of the terms of the trust regardless of whether or not the designated state has any connection with the trust."

Should You Consider a Trust?

Whether you need a revocable living trust to avoid probate depends on the state in which you live, the size of your probate estate, and which assets you're leaving to your beneficiaries. If the assets you want to leave are larger than allowed for in the following state list, then you should seriously consider a revocable living trust.

The state guidelines in the chart on the following pages are based on state laws for informal probate. Informal probate is cheaper and faster than full probate, but can usually only be used when there are no disagreements among the inheritors. Sometimes this procedure is limited to spouses and children. If your state allows informal probate, then you may not need a trust, so the dollar amounts are based on limits for informal probate. (Please note: Rules and procedures for informal probate can change; please check with your local probate court.)

That said, however, there are some additional considerations that may indicate the use of trust. Consider a trust if:

- There's a possibility that there will be beneficiaries under the age of 25.

- You have children with special needs, meaning that they will never be able to support themselves financially due to a physical or mental disability.

- You own real estate of any value in more than one state.

- Your estate is worth close to S1,000,000.

If any of these conditions apply to you, have a trust prepared by an experienced trust lawyer.

DO I NEED A REVOCABLE TRUST? STATE LIST

Alabama	Use a revocable trust if the value of the net estate exceeds $3,000.
Alaska	Use a revocable trust if the value of the net estate exceeds $15,000.
Arizona	Use a revocable trust if the value of the net estate exceeds $100,000 or real estate exceeds $50,000.
Arkansas	Use a revocable trust if you have more than a principal residence and $50,000.
California	Use a revocable trust if you have real estate worth more than $20,000 or assets other than real estate worth more than $100,000.
Colorado	Use a revocable trust if the value of the net estate exceeds $50,000.
Connecticut	Use a revocable trust if you own real estate. If you don't own real estate, use a revocable trust if the value of the net estate exceeds $20,000.
Delaware	Use a revocable trust if you own real estate. If you don't own real estate, use a revocable trust if the value of the net estate exceeds $30,000.
District of Columbia	Use a revocable trust if your assets are worth more than $40,000.
Florida	Use a revocable trust if you own real estate or the value of the net estate exceeds $75,000.
Georgia	Use a revocable trust unless you don't wish to make distributions to anyone but your heirs at law, you know that there will be no arguments, and you know you'll have no debts when you die.
Hawaii	Use a revocable trust if you own real estate or if the value of all assets other than real estate exceeds $100,000. The court will take 3 percent of assets transferred under $100,000 as a fee.

DO I NEED A REVOCABLE TRUST? STATE LIST, cont'd.

Idaho	Use a revocable trust if the value of the net estate exceeds $75,000 and there is real estate.
Illinois	Use a revocable trust if the value of the gross estate exceeds $100,000.
Indiana	Use a revocable trust if the value of the net estate exceeds $25,000.
Iowa	Use a revocable trust if the value of the net estate exceeds $50,000, or if you're leaving assets of more than $15,000 to someone other than a spouse or child.
Kansas	Use a revocable trust if the value of the net estate exceeds $20,000 and includes real estate. (The simplified probate procedures are generous in Kansas, but they depend on the approval of a judge, so there are no consistent guidelines.)
Kentucky	Use a revocable trust if the value of the net estate exceeds $15,000.
Louisiana	Use a revocable trust if you own real estate or other assets worth more than $50,000, or if you want to leave assets to someone other than a family member. (Executor gets a minimum of 2.5 percent of estate value.)
Maine	Use a revocable trust if the value of the net estate exceeds $10,000.
Maryland	Use a revocable trust if the value of the net estate exceeds $30,000.
Massachusetts	Use a revocable trust if the value of the net estate exceeds $15,000.
Michigan	Use a revocable trust if the value of the net estate exceeds $15,000.
Minnesota	Use a revocable trust if the value of the net estate exceeds $20,000 or you own real estate.

DO I NEED A REVOCABLE TRUST?
STATE LIST, cont'd.

Mississippi	Use a revocable trust if the value of the net estate exceeds $500.
Missouri	Use a revocable trust if the value of the net estate exceeds $40,000.
Montana	Use a revocable trust if the value of the net estate exceeds $50,000.
Nebraska	Use a revocable trust if the value of the net estate exceeds $25,000.
Nevada	Use a revocable trust if the value of the net estate exceeds $75,000.
New Hampshire	Use a revocable trust if the value of the net estate exceeds $10,000 or if you own real estate.
New Jersey	Use a revocable trust if the value of the net estate exceeds $10,000.
New Mexico	Use a revocable trust if the value of the net estate exceeds $30,000 or includes real estate.
New York	Use a revocable trust if the value of the net estate exceeds $20,000 or includes real estate.
North Carolina	Use a revocable trust if the value of the net estate exceeds $10,000 or includes real estate.
North Dakota	Use a revocable trust if the value of the net estate exceeds $50,000.
Ohio	Use a revocable trust if the value of the net estate exceeds $35,000.
Oklahoma	Use a revocable trust if the value of the net estate exceeds $150,000.
Oregon	Use a revocable trust if the value of the net estate exceeds $140,000 or you own real estate worth more than $90,000.

DO I NEED A REVOCABLE TRUST? STATE LIST, cont'd.

Pennsylvania	Use a revocable trust if the value of the net estate exceeds $25,000 or you own real estate.
Rhode Island	Use a revocable trust if the value of the net estate exceeds $15,000 or you own real estate.
South Carolina	Use a revocable trust if the value of the net estate exceeds $10,000.
South Dakota	Informal probate is available regardless of the value of the net estate, so use a revocable trust if there's a possibility that your beneficiaries won't agree on how to distribute your assets.
Tennessee	Use a revocable trust if the value of the net estate exceeds $25,000 or includes real estate.
Texas	Informal probate is available regardless of the value of the net estate, but inheritors must all agree. So use a revocable trust if there's a possibility that your beneficiaries won't agree on how to distribute your assets. You must also authorize an independent administrator in the will. There will still be several filings with the court for informal probate.
Utah	Use a revocable trust if the value of the net estate exceeds $25,000.
Vermont	Use a revocable trust if the value of the net estate exceeds $10,000 or includes real estate.
Virginia	Use a revocable trust if the value of the net estate exceeds $15,000 or you own real estate.

DO I NEED A REVOCABLE TRUST? STATE LIST, cont'd.

Washington	Informal probate is available regardless of the value of the net estate. Use a revocable trust if there's a possibility that your beneficiaries won't agree on how to distribute your assets. There will still be several filings with the court for informal probate.
West Virginia	Use a revocable trust if the value of the net estate exceeds $100,000 or you own real estate.
Wisconsin	Use a revocable trust if the value of the net estate exceeds $50,000 or if you're leaving assets to someone other than a spouse or a child.
Wyoming	Use a revocable trust if the value of the net estate exceeds $150,000.

- *What is a revocable living trust?* A revocable living trust is a written document stating who controls your assets while you're still alive (typically, you) and what will happen to those assets once you're gone. It's called "revocable" because you can change it at any time, "living" because you create and fund it while you're alive, and a "trust" because you entrust it with the title to your property. Its purpose is to hold your assets while you live, and carry out your wishes when you can no longer do so for yourself.

- *How is a revocable living trust different from a will?* Revocable trusts are an increasingly popular alternative to wills. Although a will states who you want your assets to go after your death, it takes effect only with a court order. With a revocable living trust, the court is removed from the equation. You take the necessary actions while you're alive to pass assets directly to your beneficiaries once you die. You do this by signing the title of your assets over to the trust. The property is held in your name as trustee for *your* trust—and for your benefit while you live. You can always add things to the trust, take things out of it, and amend it if you change your mind about who you wish to get what. When you die, the trust passes your property directly to the people you want to have it—and it does so without probate.

• *What's the cost of a revocable living trust?* Depending on the size of your estate, you should be able to get a simple revocable living trust drawn up by an attorney for between $500 and $3,000. If you decide you want the attorney to fund the trust—that is, to transfer your assets into it—it might cost you more. Once the trust is set up, making simple changes to it should cost about $200. Obviously, fees will vary depending on the state where you live and how complex your requirements are.

TERMINOLOGY OF TRUSTS

Term	Definition
Beneficiary	A person or organization designated to receive your assets upon your death.
Current Beneficiary	The person or persons for whom all assets are being held in trust.
Estate	The sum total of your financial interests, both money and property. Your estate is made up of everything you own at the time of your death, including life insurance, less your outstanding debt.
Remainder Beneficiaries	The person or persons who will inherit everything in the trust after the current beneficiary (who is usually the trustor as well) dies.
Successor Trustee	The person who steps in to make decisions about the assets in the trust if and only if the trustee or co-trustees can't or don't want to act in the decision-making process.
Settlor, Trustor, or Grantor	The person who creates a trust and owns the property that will be put into the trust.
Trustee	The person or group of persons who control the assets in the trust. Most often the trustor is also the trustee. When you set up a trust, you don't have to give away your power over your assets. Most people continue taking care of everything just as they did before the trust existed.

Funding Your Trust

Funding your trust means transferring ownership of your assets to the trust. By itself, your trust document means nothing; it's only when your trust assumes ownership of the things you intend to put into it that it becomes a valid legal tool. So to avoid probate, you must transfer the titles of all major assets, such as real estate, stocks, savings accounts, bonds, and limited partnerships, to the trust. This should be done as soon as is practical after the trust is signed.

Funding your trust is all a simple matter of paperwork, but since different institutions have different procedures for changing title, it may be advantageous to have your lawyer handle it for you. A thorough attorney will update the beneficiary designations on your life-insurance policies, IRAs, and other retirement accounts at the same time.

Here's an example of funding a trust: Let's say that John and Jane Doe own a house together in their own names. They decide to create and fund a trust to hold the title to their house and other assets. After they've established the trust, they record a new deed that lists the owners of the house as *John and Jane Doe, Trustees of the John and Jane Doe Revocable Trust.* The house would then be "in" the trust. The Does would also change the titles on their bank accounts, stock-brokerage accounts, and other assets so that these are also held by the trust.

On the Protection Portfolio CD-ROM, you'll find forms you can use to fund your trust. As you're listening to the information on the CD-ROM, you may find that you have additional questions about funding a trust, so the following section is a resource devoted to common questions about funding a trust.

In addition to the information supplied on the CD-ROM, I've listed the following revocable trust benefit statement definitions in this guidebook to help you make the choice on how you want your assets distributed (these choices will be presented on the CD-ROM program when you create your revocable trust).

REVOCABLE TRUST BENEFICIARY STATEMENT DEFINITIONS	
Term	**Definition**
Parent Support	In order to plan for the possibility that an adult child may die before a parent or parents, we've provided the opportunity for you to set aside certain funds within the trust that can be used to help support an elderly parent or parents without making them ineligible for possible public benefits. If you use this choice, the parent beneficiary may not serve as your Trustee or Successor Trustee.
Right of Representation	This statement means that if the beneficiary you've named dies before you do, then you want the share that beneficiary would have taken to go to their child, children, or lineal descendants.
Equal Shares to Lapse	This statement means that if one of the beneficiaries dies before you, then their share goes away—it doesn't go to their children. So if you give equal shares to seven nieces and nephews and one dies before you, then there will just be six shares, even if the deceased nephew had his own children.
Percentages	This statement means that you can choose to distribute your estate in amounts designated by percentages. This allows you to distribute your estate into equal or unequal shares and between individuals and organizations.

REVOCABLE TRUST BENEFICIARY STATEMENT DEFINITIONS, cont'd.

Term	Definition
Specific Gifts	This statement allows a beneficiary to be named to receive a specific gift, such as your home. Specific gifts are usually not the best idea—since most people don't know when they're going to die, there may be unintended consequences when leaving a specific asset to someone. The asset may have been sold before you die leaving the beneficiary with nothing. You may have spent all your other assets, leaving other beneficiaries with nothing. However, there are cases where it's very clear that a specific asset should be given to a specific beneficiary.

- *What is the legal title of my revocable living trust?* When you fund your trust, the legal title of your transferred assets must be changed. So instead of holding title as [YOUR FULL NAME], the new title will be: *[YOUR FULL NAME] as Trustee of the [YOUR FULL NAME] Revocable Trust.* Or, if you and your spouse have created a trust together, you'd hold title as *[YOUR FULL NAME] and [SPOUSE'S FULL NAME] as Trustees of the [YOUR FULL NAME] and [SPOUSE'S FULL NAME] Revocable Trust.*

  Although the terms *revocable living trust* and *revocable trust* are used interchangeably in the Protection Portfolio materials, *revocable trust* is the recognized legal description and should be used in the title of your trust documents. You can be identified as the trustor, grantor, and/or settlor of the trust, and you're also the trustee. If you're married, you and your spouse are the beneficiaries of the trust while you're living.

- *What is the date of my revocable living trust?* The date you sign the trust in front of a notary public and have it notarized becomes the date of your trust, also known as Under Declaration of Trust Dated, or UDT. Even if you restate your trust at a later time, the original signature date will always be the legal date of the trust.

  The UDT is very important because it's often used to identify the trust. Financial institutions often request this date when you fill out the funding documents for your trust, and you'll also need it to complete the funding documents on your Protection Portfolio CD-ROM.

- *What tax identification number should I use for the trust?* The tax identification number that's used for your revocable living trust is your Social Security number. Married couples should choose either, but not both, of their numbers for the trust. If the settlor whose Social Security number is being used for the trust dies, change the trust assets to the surviving settlor's Social Security number by contacting your financial institutions.

- *How are the titles of my bank, brokerage, and credit-union accounts and safe-deposit box listed in the revocable living trust?* Many people want to keep their original trust and will in a safe-deposit box in case of fire. The title to the box and to your bank accounts—including checking and savings accounts, mutual funds, and certificate of deposit accounts (or CDs)—should be the legal title of your trust. You can use the Protection Portfolio CD-ROM to create the forms "Mutual Funds Change of Ownership Letter" and "Bank and Credit-Union Instruction Letter" to change the title to your accounts.

- *Are stocks put in a revocable living trust?* If you hold stock certificates, you'll need to have new certificates issued in the legal name of the trust. The transfer agent from the company who issued the stock will provide the new certificates. The name of the transfer agent should be listed on the stock certificate, but if it isn't, you can contact the investor relations department of the issuing company. Complete and print the form "Request to Transfer Stock Ownership" from your Protection Portfolio CD-ROM to request the change of ownership.

- *Should I put real property in a revocable living trust?* The only way to change title to real property is by recording a deed in the office of the County Recorder where the property is located. When you purchase new property, take title in the name of your trust so that the property will be in the trust from the beginning.

It's important to consult a local real-estate lawyer or title company to ensure that the deeds are created specifically for your location. Different states, and even counties within the same state, have specific requirements that must appear in the deed to preserve homestead exemptions and property-tax rates. The cost is usually around $125 to transfer each deed.

When requesting that the property title be changed to the title of your trust, you'll want to take the following documents to your local title company:

— Grant deed for each property

— Property-tax statement

— The cover and signature page of your trust or a certification of trust

When transferring real estate into the trust, make sure that you as the trustee are named as the insured on the property-insurance policy. Contact your homeowners-insurance agent and inform him or her of the change to ensure that your property is covered under the policy.

• *Do I need to change the name on my title insurance?* When you first obtained title insurance for your property, your name was on the title and you were the named insured. Once you transfer title to the trust, there is a new title holder—that is, the trust.

Some newer title policies automatically provide coverage for trustees of the trust under the continuation of coverage provisions of the policy, but most older ones don't. Check your policy to see whether it gives such coverage already. If it doesn't, or you aren't sure if it does, call your title company and ask them. If they inform you that your policy doesn't cover the trustee, then a simple endorsement to the policy is available (for a nominal fee), which will offer such coverage. Purchase the endorsement and you'll be covered.

- *What if I have business interests, partnerships, and LLCs?* The title to all such accounts should be *[YOUR FULL NAME] as Trustee of the [YOUR FULL NAME] Revocable Trust* for a single person, or *[YOUR FULL NAME] and [SPOUSE FULL NAME] as Trustees of the [YOUR FULL NAME] and [SPOUSE FULL NAME] Revocable Trust* for a married couple. You can use the forms "Assignment of Business Interests," "Assignment of Limited Partnership Interest," and/or "Amendment to the [Company Name] LLC" on your Protection Portfolio CD-ROM to change the ownership of these accounts.

- *What do I do if I have promissory notes?* If you hold a promissory note signed by someone who owes you money, the note can be assigned to the trust by endorsing the back of the note as follows:

I assign my interest in the within promissory note to [YOUR FULL NAME] as Trustee of the [YOUR FULL NAME] Revocable Trust or in the married legal title as stated earlier.

_____

(signature)

Dated:_____
(date of assignment)

You should advise the payor of the note to make future payments to you in your name as trustee(s). Secured notes should be assigned by a formal assignment that's recorded in the same manner as the original trust deed.

- *Do I put pension plans, IRAs, life insurance, and annuities in a revocable living trust?* These investments make direct payments to the named beneficiary, so they already avoid probate. However, I still recommend that you change the named beneficiary to the trust so that all of the protections of the trust apply to these assets as well. If you're single, name your trust as the primary beneficiary. If you're married, name your spouse as the primary beneficiary and the trust as the contingent beneficiary. This designation will give your spouse the greatest income-tax protection.

  To name or change beneficiaries, request designation of beneficiary forms from your insurance company, company pension plan, or the company administering your IRA or pension plan, or you can use the "IRA Beneficiary Designation Form" on the Protection Portfolio CD-ROM.

- *Do I put automobiles in a revocable living trust?* It's not necessary to transfer automobiles into the trust (unless they're expensive investment-type cars), and transferring the title to the trust can cause confusion with registration and insurance. Most states permit transfers of automobile title by affidavit at the time of death. This form should be available from your state's Department of Motor Vehicles.

- *How do I provide for children with a trust?* If you have children, then the earlier you create your revocable living trust, the better. That's true even if you don't have a lot of money. If your children are very young and something were to happen to you, they might be at greater risk than you imagine. A court always has the last word when it comes to who is appointed legal guardian of your children—a will can only express your wishes. So, for example, if your children are under 18 and all you leave them is a life-insurance policy, a guardianship for those assets will be created upon your death. Each year the guardian will have to go back to court to account for the money spent on behalf of the children. When each child reaches 18, that child's share will be legally signed over to him or her—lock, stock, and barrel—regardless of his or her ability to handle the money. But by the time the children get the money, there won't be as much of it as there could have been, since every year there will have been guardian fees and payments to a lawyer to do the guardianship reporting. These fees are usually in the thousands of dollars.

Trusts don't address the issue of guardianship—you need a will for that. But if you die with a trust, you do get to make the important decision of how, when, and for what purposes your children will receive the money you're leaving them. You can assign one or more successor trustees (your chosen guardian, for example) and instruct them to carry out your wishes as to when your children should receive their money and how that money should he used until that time—and poof, it's done. The successor trustee(s) can take care of your children's financial lives on your behalf. No yearly court reporting, no fees.

- *Will a revocable living trust help me with estate taxes?* No. A revocable living trust won't help with the estate taxes on estates whose value rises above the unified credit exemption (see page 57 for more information on the unified credit exemption). A revocable living trust is primarily helpful in transferring legal title to your assets as quickly as possible to beneficiaries, eliminating probate fees, and protecting you when you become incapacitated by providing for a smooth transition of management from you to your successor trustee without the need for court involvement.

- *I'm part of a blended family. Is a revocable living trust still the best way for me to protect my family?* Due to the number of blended families that exist, I've included a blended family version of the revocable living trust on the Protection Portfolio CD-ROM. The blended family trust is designed to allow you to combine assets during your joint lifetimes. If you use the blended family trust, all assets transferred to the trust are then owned equally by both you and your spouse. You each have the right to leave your half the way you want when you die.

  So, for example, if you were to die before your spouse, you could leave one half of the assets in the trust to be distributed to the beneficiaries that you choose, while the other half of the assets would remain in the trust for the benefit of your surviving spouse. You could also choose to leave part of your half to your children and the other part of your half to your spouse.

NEED TO KNOW

If you have concerns that your spouse might rewrite your blended family trust to diminish your children's share of your joint estate or leave them with nothing after you pass away, please see an attorney to develop a trust that will create an irrevocable trust share at your death. Even if you decide not to combine assets and each of you complete a separate trust, if you leave your estate—in part or in full—to your surviving spouse, she can then bequeath those assets to whomever she wants at her death.

- *What happens if I become incapacitated or disabled?* Your revocable living trust provides the language to allow the person that you choose to determine whether you're "incompetent" or "disabled" to the extent that you're unable to carry out your usual business affairs. This person can be your child or another person of your choosing, and isn't required to involve the courts in the determination. This process allows you to decide who will make this very important decision.

  Once the determination of incapacity has been signed, in order for the successor trustee to take over the management of the trust, he or she will need to change the title of the assets of the trust into the name of the successor trustee. The successor trustee will then need to contact your financial institutions and let them know that the trustee of your trust has changed and ask for their procedure for updating your paperwork. Each financial institution has different requirements, so find out what they need and if they have a form available for you to use.

  The Protection Portfolio CD-ROM provides a form that can be used for the determination of incapacity. Be sure to keep the original determination of incapacity form with your trust and send a duplicate copy if your bank or other financial institution asks you to provide one.

- *How do I resign as the trustee of the revocable living trust?* You may decide that you no longer want to serve as the trustee of your revocable living trust, and that you want to have your successor trustee take over the management for you. This is a simple procedure of stating the facts as they appear in your trust and having the document notarized. Once you have the resignation form finalized, your successor trustee can contact your financial institutions and let them know that the trustee of your trust has changed, and ask for their procedure for updating your paperwork. Each financial institution has different requirements, so find out what they need and if they have a form available for you to use.

On the Protection Portfolio CD-ROM is a form that can be used for the resignation of a trustee. Be sure to keep the original resignation form with your trust and include a duplicate copy in case you're required to provide a copy of the trust to the bank or other financial institution.

- *What does a successor trustee need to do first?* The first step is to contact the financial institutions and let them know that the trustee of the revocable living trust has changed. The successor trustee will need to have the assets of the trust transferred to the new name of the trust: *[SUCCESSOR TRUSTEE NAME], Trustee of the [YOUR FULL NAME] Revocable Trust.* This transfer needs to occur so that the successor trustee has access to the assets. The bank or financial institution should have an established procedure and may require you to complete their form to make the transfer.

- *What is a certification of trust?* A certification of trust is used to identify the basic information about your trust, the trustees, beneficiaries, and authorized agents, along with guidelines for authorized transactions. Your financial institution may request a certification of trust instead of a copy of your trust when processing the transfer of your accounts. The details contained in this form must match the language contained in your trust and any amendments to the trust, such as a resignation of trustee and appointment of a successor trustee.

    On your Protection Portfolio CD-ROM a form is provided that can be used for the certification of trust. Be sure to keep the original certification of trust form with your trust and retain a duplicate copy in case you're ever requested to provide a copy of the trust to your bank or other financial institution.

- *What is the unified credit exemption?* The unified credit exemption is the amount that your beneficiaries can inherit from you without having to pay federal estate taxes, as follows:

    According to the Economic Growth and Tax Relief Reconciliation Act of 2001, estate taxes are being phased out over nine years, beginning in 2002. According to the law as it now stands, if you die in the year 2010 there will be no estate tax due on your estate, no matter what its size; and the top gift-tax rate will be equal to the highest individual income-tax rate (scheduled to be 35 percent), with a $1 million unified credit exemption. But please keep in mind that unless new legislation is passed, in 2011 the act will expire, and estate taxes, along with the highest unified credit exemption, will be reinstated at the 2001 rate.

UNIFIED CREDIT EXEMPTION

For Deaths Occurring In	Highest Estate Exemption	Highest Estate & Gift-Tax Rate
2008	$2,000,000	45%
2009	$3,500,000	45%

- *Is there any trust that reduces estate taxes?* Yes. An A-B trust (also known as a tax-planning trust, a credit-shelter trust, a marital trust, or a bypass trust) reduces estate taxes. If you have close to $1 million in assets, I urge you to see a trust attorney about an A-B trust.

- *How do I find a good will and trust attorney?* Finding a good will and trust attorney is the hardest part of creating a will and a trust. Word of mouth is the age-old method of choice, so ask your friends for recommendations—but please be certain that the attorney you choose is well versed in estate planning. If your friends can't recommend a qualified attorney, you might want to contact your local university, especially if it has a law school. Call a professor who specializes in estate planning and ask whom he or she would recommend.

Alternately, you can consult this professional organization:

> The American College of Trust and
> Estate Counsel
> 3415 S. Sepulveda Blvd., Ste. 460
> Los Angeles, CA 90034
> 310-398-1888
> 310-572-7280 (fax)
> *www.actec.org*

After you've collected some names, please make sure you interview at least three attorneys before you settle on one. Good attorneys are usually too busy for full interviews, but most will give you an interview by phone. An attorney will play a major role in making sure your estate is set up correctly, and your survivor will need his or her assistance after your death, so you'll want to be sure that not only you but also those around you like this lawyer and feel comfortable in his or her presence.

How to Interview a Will and Trust Attorney

Ask a prospective attorney the following questions, and be sure you get the following answers before going further. If you get another answer, you haven't found the right attorney:

- *How long have you been specializing in estate planning?* The only acceptable answer is at least ten years.

- *What other areas of law do you practice?* The answer should be no other areas.

- *How many people have you drafted wills and trusts for in the past five years?* The only acceptable answer is at least 200 people.

- *Will you be drafting the documents yourself, or will someone else be doing the paperwork?* It's okay if someone else draws up the documents, as long as that person is supervised correctly. In fact, this arrangement may cost you less. You just need to know one way or the other.

- *How much do you charge?* You want the attorney to charge a flat fee to draw up a will and/or a trust. The fee should include drafting and explaining the document (which could take a few hours if it's a trust), as well as funding the trust (doing the paperwork to transfer the titles on all your property and assets into the name of the trust).

- *If I have other questions, will you charge me if I call and ask?* There should be no charge for simple questions over the phone.

On your Protection Portfolio CD-ROM, you'll find a worksheet to use when you're interviewing prospective attorneys. Remember, you'll need to interview at least three attorneys before you decide on one.

Final Instructions

Final Instructions

To carefully prepare for your death is a supreme act of love toward those you'll one day leave behind. It can be of great emotional help to your survivors, because having to deal with practical chaos after a death makes the loss itself more painful and frightening. It can also help your loved ones financially, because careful estate planning may save them thousands of dollars in probate fees, estate taxes, and attorney's fees.

By having a will and a trust, you've helped to ensure that your family members will be taken care of financially. Now take the time to prepare your final instructions so that you can help protect them emotionally as well.

Please review the "Final Instructions" form on the following page. You can also find a copy of "Final Instructions" on your Protection Portfolio forms CD-ROM. Be sure to fill out the form and place a copy in your Protection Portfolio so that your family will be aware of your last wishes.

FINAL INSTRUCTIONS FORM

Name _____

Memorial Service
    __ At home
    __ At place of worship
    __ At funeral home
    __ Other_____

Disposition of Remains
    __ Burial
    __ Cremation
    __ Embalming
    __ No embalming
    __ Open casket
    __ Closed casket

Funeral Home Preference
    Company:_____
    Address:_____
    Telephone: _____
    Contact: _____

Cemetery Preference
    Company: _____
    Address: _____
    Telephone: _____
    Contact: _____

Documentation of Prepayment (please attach any paid receipts or contracts to this form)
    __ Memorial service
    __ Funeral
    __ Cemetery
    __ Burial plot

Special Instructions

_____
_____
_____

Claiming Benefits

If you're the one left behind in the event of a death, you'll need to look into claiming benefits. Chances are good that your spouse or life partner had a number of policies or accounts with benefits that you may be eligible for. Please check these thoroughly, following the instructions provided here for each type of benefit.

Social Security Benefits

If the deceased had paid into Social Security for at least 40 quarters, two types of benefits are possible—a death benefit or survivors benefits. You can apply for either one by telephone or in person at any Social Security office.

Death benefits provide qualified spouses or dependent children with $255 for burial expenses. Survivors can complete the necessary form at a local Social Security office, or a funeral director may complete the application and apply the payment directly to the funeral bill.

Those who are eligible for survivors benefits have a variety of benefits available to them, depending on their age and relationship with the deceased. You may be eligible for survivors benefits if you match any of these descriptions:

- You're a spouse, age 60 or older

- You're a disabled surviving spouse, age 50 or older

- You're a spouse under 60 who cares for dependent children under 16, or for disabled children

- You're a child of the deceased under the age of 18, or a child who is disabled

If you're not already receiving Social Security benefits at the time of your loved one's death, here are some other points to keep in mind:

- Apply promptly for survivors benefits. In some cases, benefits may not be retroactive.

- Try to have the necessary information close at hand, but don't panic if you don't have it. Social Security will ask for specific information and documents in order to process your application. It's helpful if you have the right forms when you apply, but don't delay applying if you don't have everything. You'll need either original documents or copies certified by the agency that issued them. These will include:

  - Proof of death, either from funeral home or a death certificate

  - Your Social Security number, as well as the worker's

  - Your birth certificate

  - Your marriage certificate, if you're a widow or widower of the deceased

  - Your divorce papers, if you're applying as a surviving divorced spouse

  - Dependent children's Social Security numbers, if available

- Deceased worker's W-2 forms or federal self-employment tax return for the most recent year

- The name of your bank and your account number, so that benefits can be directly deposited into your account

If you're already getting Social Security benefits as a wife or husband on your spouse's record at the time of his or her death, you should report the death to the Social Security Administration, which will change your payments to survivors benefits.

If you're getting benefits on your own record, you'll need to complete an application to get survivors benefits. Call or visit your local Social Security office and an official will check to see if you can get more money as a widow or widower. To process your claim, Social Security needs to see a certified copy of your spouse's death certificate.

Benefits for any children will automatically be changed to survivors benefits after the death is reported to Social Security.

How Much Will You Get?

The amount of your Social Security benefit is based on the earnings of the person who died. The more he or she paid into Social Security, the higher your benefits will be. The amount you'll get is a percentage of the deceased's basic Social Security benefit. The percentage depends on your age and the type of benefit you're eligible for. Here are the most typical situations:

- Widow or widower, age 65 or older: 100 percent

- Widow or widower, age 60 to 64: about 71 to 94 percent

- Widow, any age, with a child under age 16: 75 percent

- Children: 75 percent

There's a limit to the total amount of money that can be paid to you and other family members each month. The limit varies, but is typically equal to about 150 to 180 percent of the deceased's benefit rate. If the sum of the benefits payable to the family members is greater than this limit, the benefits will be reduced proportionately.

Veterans Benefits

If your loved one was already receiving monthly payments from the Department of Veterans Affairs (VA), you'll need to notify them of the death.

If the deceased was a veteran, he or she may be eligible for burial in one of the 115 national cemeteries, free of charge. Veterans assistance may provide transportation of the remains to the nearest veterans cemetery and a marker or headstone, as well as a flag. If you choose a veterans burial, you'll have to document the fact that the deceased was a veteran, including his or her separation papers (in the "Personal Documents" section of the Protection Portfolio CD-ROM, you'll find a link to request a copy of these military records), and have proof of rank and branch of the service, date of entry into and date of departure from the service, date of birth, date of death, Social Security number (his or hers, as well as your own), and name and address of the executor or trustee of the estate.

If you use a private cemetery, you still can apply for a burial allowance, flag, and a government headstone or marker from the VA. To apply, just look in the blue pages of your phone book for the number of the VA office nearest you, For more information, log on to *www.cem.va.gov*.

Employee Benefits

Many employers provide life, health, or accident insurance that you may be eligible to make a claim against or continue after the death of your loved one. Additionally, the deceased may be due a final paycheck for vacation or sick leave. Be sure to contact all past employers, include federal, state, or local governments, to see if you're entitled to death benefits, continued health-insurance coverage for the family, or payments from an annuity or pension plan. If the deceased belonged to a union or professional organization, check to see if it offers death benefits for members.

Funeral and Burial Costs

Funerals and burials are among the most expensive purchases older people make. The average cost of a traditional funeral is $7,323. A large part of this cost is for embalming, which you should know isn't required by law unless you're transporting a body across state lines. Viewings are possible even if you choose not to be embalmed, and the funeral home will refrigerate the body for a minimal fee (or no fee at all). Be sure to ask about this option.

Additional costs such as flowers, obituary notices, acknowledgment cards, burial liners or vaults, and special transportation can add an additional $1,000. In-ground burial costs at least another $2,400. Some of the services you're likely to be offered and/or charged for include:

- Funeral-director services for initial conference, consultations, paperwork, and overhead (this fee is added to all bills)

- Transportation of the body to the funeral home and to the place of final disposition

- Care of the body, including embalming and "casketing," or dressing the body

- Cremation

- Use of facilities for a viewing, wake, or visitation, and the funeral or memorial ceremony at the funeral home

- Purchasing flowers

- Preparing obituary notices

- Providing music

Traditionally, caskets were sold only by funeral homes. Today, however, cemeteries and third parties sell caskets—even on the Internet. Collect price lists from several funeral homes to compare costs of a particular model. Under the federal Funeral Rule, a funeral home can't charge you extra if you provide your own casket from an outside source. No casket is required if you choose direct cremation, immediate burial, or to donate the body to science.

A grave liner or vault is an outer burial container that surround the casket in the grave to prevent the ground from sinking, as settling occurs over time. In many locations, both funeral homes and cemeteries sell vaults and liners. In some areas it's possible, and less expensive, to purchase an outer burial container from a third party. You can collect outer burial container price lists from several providers to compare the costs of a particular model. (Keep in mind that even if you've already purchased a burial plot, you'll most likely be charged an opening fee when the time comes to use the plot.)

The term "immediate burial" refers to a simple, low-cost funeral. The body is interred without embalming, usually in a simple container. There is no viewing or ceremony with the body present. A package price for immediate burial will include the funeral director's fee, transportation, and care of the body. It may not include the charge for a container, casket, or simple pine box.

If you choose a direct cremation package, the price usually includes the funeral director's fee and transportation and care of the body. It may not include the charge for cremation.

NEED TO KNOW

The Funeral Rule requires funeral homes to provide price lists so that you know what options are available to you and exactly how much they'll cost. Funeral homes, but not cemeteries, must disclose prices by telephone and offer price lists for review at each facility. Many funeral homes will mail you a price list, although the law doesn't require this. To obtain a copy of the Funeral Rule, call 877-FTC-HELP or log on to *www.ftc.gov/bcp/rulemaking/funeral*.

Most of us are unprepared to make wise financial decisions about a funeral and burial. We have little or no experience with making funeral arrangements. The emotions surrounding the death of a loved one—or contemplating our own mortality, if we're prearranging our own funeral—may cloud our judgment. It's never easy to make funeral and burial arrangements, but finding out about them in advance is easier than coping with them at a time of need. If you want to know everything about the funeral industry, read Jessica Mitford's book *The American Way of Death Revisited*. It's very informative and humorous. In the meantime, here are some pointers:

- *Shop around for the best prices.* Most of us select a funeral home or cemetery based on location, reputation, or personal experience. There's nothing wrong with that, but you may pay too much if you only call one facility. Call or visit at least two funeral homes and cemeteries to compare prices.

- *Compare prices for the entire package, not just a single item.* Every funeral home should have separate price lists for general services, caskets, and outer burial containers. Only by using all three lists can you accurately find the total costs and be able to compare prices.

  Use the "Funeral-Home Cost" worksheet on your Protection Portfolio CD-ROM to help compare your findings.

- *Be sure you buy only what you planned to buy.* Try to keep in mind that the amount you spend on a funeral and burial isn't a reflection of your feelings for the deceased.

WHAT TO DO WHEN SOMEONE YOU LOVE DIES

_____ In the Estate Planning Documents folder in your Protection Portfolio, locate your loved one's final instructions form.

_____ If death took place in the hospital, you'll be asked the name of the funeral home or cremation society of your choice, which will then make arrangements to transport the remains. Find out how much they'll charge to transport the body.

_____ If death took place at your home or anywhere other than a hospital, then you have to contact the funeral home or cremation society of your choice, which will make the arrangement to transport the remains. Find out how much they'll charge to transport the body.

_____ If you don't know which funeral home you want to use, ask your friends, your clergyman, or the local coroner.

_____ Ask a close friend or family member to help notify family and friends of the death of your loved one.

_____ Make funeral, burial, or cremation arrangements. Be clear about embalming, as it's expensive and not required by law.

_____ Order at least 15 certified copies of the death certificate. You'll need them in order to collect insurance proceeds and to change the name on bank accounts, deeds, and other assets.

_____ Try not to leave the house vacant, as this may have consequences for insurance coverage. Call the insurance broker to make sure coverage continues.

WHAT TO DO WHEN
SOMEONE YOU LOVE DIES, cont'd.

_____ If you don't already have one, open a bank account in your own name.

_____ If you don't have a credit card in your own name, request one. After you've received your own card and credit limit, advise the credit-card company of your loved one's death.

_____ Before paying any credit-card debts that aren't yours, check with your attorney or executor. If there isn't enough money in the estate to pay off the debts, the probate has a "schedule" specifying debts given priority and the order in which the debts are to be paid—which is why I want you to check with your attorney before you begin paying the debts.

_____ Go to your Protection Portfolio and remove your loved one's insurance policy. In addition to life insurance, check to see if other forms of insurance covered the deceased. Some loans, mortgages, and credit-card accounts are covered by credit life insurance, which pays off account balances. Contact each insurance company about how to claim the policy benefits.

_____ Contact your local Social Security, Veterans Administration, and deceased's employer's human resource office, or visit their Websites to see if there are any benefits you qualify for.

_____ Your own will or trust should be changed now, for most likely you left everything to the person who has just died. Make sure you change the beneficiary designation on your IRA, life-insurance policies, pension plans, 401(k) plans, and other investment or retirement plans.

Begin Today

Thinking about your own death or the death of a family member is no easy task—neither is contemplating serious illness or incapacity. But planning for your future doesn't have to be a morbid subject. In fact, it can, and probably will, provide you with a sense of control over your own life. It's freeing to know that you've protected those you care about the most.

If you plan carefully, you and your family can save thousands of dollars in probate fees, estate taxes, and attorney fees, as well as spare yourselves the nuisance of going through an unnecessarily complicated and lengthy probate process. In my experience, once you've begun to take steps to protect your future and the futures of the people you care about, you'll have started down the path toward securing your own financial freedom.

About the Author

Suze Orman has written six consecutive *New York Times* best-sellers: *Women & Money; The Money Book for the Young, Fabulous & Broke; The Laws of Money, The Lessons of Life; The Road to Wealth; The Courage to Be Rich;* and *The 9 Steps to Financial Freedom,* as well as the national bestsellers, *Suze Orman's Financial Guidebook* and *You've Earned It, Don't Lose It.* In addition, she has created Suze Orman's Identity Theft Kit, *Suze Orman's FICO Kit, Suze Orman's Will & Trust Kit, Suze Orman's Insurance Kit, The Ask Suze Library System* and *Suze Orman's Ultimate Protection Portfolio.*

Orman has written, co-produced, and hosted six PBS specials based on her *New York Times* best-selling books, and she is the single most successful fundraiser in the history of public television. She twice won a Daytime Emmy Award in the category of Outstanding Service Show Host, and her latest PBS Special "Women & Money" began airing nationwide on PBS in March 2007.

Orman is a contributing editor to *O, The Oprah Magazine* in the United States and South Africa and to *O at Home.* She has a bi-weekly column, *Money Matters,* on Yahoo! Finance, and writes a syndicated newspaper column entitled *Women & Money.* Suze hosts the award-winning *The Suze Orman Show,* which airs every Saturday night on CNBC and on XM & Sirus radio, and also hosts the *Financial Freedom Hour* on QVC television. In September 2007, Hay House Radio began airing Suze's radio show, *The Spirit of Wealth.*

Orman, a CERTIFIED FINANCIAL PLANNER™ professional, directed the Suze Orman Financial Group from 1987–1997, served as Vice President of Investments for Prudential Bache Securities from 1983–87, and from 1980–83 was an Account Executive at Merrill Lynch. Prior to that, she worked as a waitress at the Buttercup Bakery in Berkeley, California, from 1973–80.